Fish and Seafood

From caviar to grouper, mussels, salmon and shrimp
From filleting to poaching and portioning

© 2004 Feierabend Verlag OHG
Mommsenstr. 43, D-10629 Berlin

Concept: Peter Feierabend
Recipes, Styling, Production: Patrik Jaros
Copy and editorial assistance: Martina Dürkop
Photography: Günter Beer – food.beerfoto.com
Assistant: Kathrin Günter
Additional assistance: Bamboo
Photographed in BuenavistaStudio.com, Barcelona
Layout: Kathrin Günter

Coordination, editing and setting of the English edition:
Equipo de Edición, S.L., Barcelona
Translation from German: Amanda T. Warren

© 2004 Photography, recipes:
Günter Beer, Patrik Jaros, Feierabend Verlag OHG

Printing and Binding: Eurolitho s.p.a., Milan
Printed in Italy
ISBN 3-89985-073-4
61-08068-1

Important: all ingredients – especially fish and seafood – should
be fresh and in perfect conditions. Lettuces must be washed very
carefully. Those vulnerable to Salmonella enteritidis infecctions – in
particular the elderly, pregnant women, young children and those
with weakened immune systems – should consult their doctor before
consuming raw eggs, raw fish or seafood.

Patrik Jaros • Günter Beer

Fish and Seafood

**From caviar to grouper, mussels, salmon and shrimp
From filleting to poaching and portioning**

Feierabend

Contents

Level of difficulty   Preparation time

Introduction

The seas of the world all flow into its fish markets. They offer an extensive variety of fresh seafood and fish in a hitherto unknown abundance which continually challenges chefs' skills and fantasies. Large fish, small fish, crab, mussels, shellfish, algae, sea urchins, prawns – each desiring to be prepared freshly and flavoursome whether as a classic, modern, exotic, Asian or Italian dish.

Octopus is coated with coconut and scewered on kebab sticks, and the time-honoured cod is prepared in a papaya curry. Additionally, the dishes we all got to know on holiday such as fried sardines and the beloved bouillabaisse with Rouille all feature here. Salmon is presented in a new light wrapped in ham and on a bed of spinach, while brill appears deep-fried as traditional fish and chips. Those who prefer exotic cuisine should try the creole style skate with couscous.

The ways to prepare fish and seafood are as manifold and as diverse, as the worlds' cuisines.

This fish recipe book from the master chef Patrik Jaros fuses this culinary variety, as well as offering both simpler recipes for beginners who want to enjoy the art of cooking, plus deeper knowledge and complicated recipes for the more experienced cook. Every fish lover, including gourmets, will find inspiration here.

We hope all fish and seafood lovers will enjoy creating these recipes.

Fillet of salmon on radish salad with chive vinaigrette

8 salmon fillet strips 80 g / 3 oz each

30 g butter / 1 oz

2 bunches of radishes

1 bunch of chives

4 tbsp cider vinegar

1 tsp powdered icing sugar

1 mocha spoon Dijon mustard

6 tbsp sunflower oil

Sea salt
Freshly ground white pepper

Remove the radish leaves and cut the radishes into thin slices. Marinate the radishes in a vinaigrette of cider vinegar, powdered sugar, Dijon mustard, sea salt, white pepper and sunflower oil, and mix in the finely chopped chives. Arrange on plates.
Heat and froth the butter in a non-stick pan and add the salmon fillets. Season with sea salt and sauté each side for 1 minute. The salmon should remain moist inside. Place on the bed of radish salad and serve.

TIP
Serve either with fresh white bread or with small boiled potatoes. The slightly sharp radish salad tastes wonderful with the delicate salmon.

Boiled whelks with aioli

1 kg / approx. 2 lb whelks

½ fennel bulb, cubed
¼ celery root, cubed
1 carrot, peeled and cubed
2 cloves garlic, unpeeled

3 bay leaves
2 sprigs of thyme

½ tsp black peppercorns
1 tbsp coarse sea salt

3 litres / 96 fl oz / 12 cups water

Aioli – see recipe on page 68

Rinse and clean whelks for ½ hour under running water. In the meantime, bring the diced vegetables and spices to boil in a large pot of water and then let it simmer for 5 minutes.
Drain the whelks and add to the vegetable broth. Let them simmer for approximately 15 minutes, depending on the size of the whelks.
Remove the whelks from the broth with a slotted spoon and place them in a large bowl. Serve with aioli and toothpicks.

TIP
The opening of a whelk is sealed with a thin layer of skin. Remove it with a toothpick, then poke and pull out the whelk.
Do not eat the darker end, as it could taste somewhat bitter.
Dip in aioli and eat with white bread.

This is how to remove the delicious whelk from its shell: use a toothpick to pull it out and then dip it in the aioli.

Three ways to prepare prawns

Three ways to prepare prawns

**Sautéed prawns with garlic
and parsley**

20 prawns, fresh and with head

2 small cloves of garlic, finely chopped

½ bunch of flat-leaf parsley, finely chopped

1 lemon peel, sliced in thin strips

5 tbsp extra virgin olive oil

Sea salt
Freshly ground black pepper

50 ml / 1 ½ fl oz / ¼ cup water or fish stock

Wash the prawns and let them dry on paper
towels. Place them in a ceramic bowl. Put all
the ingredients except for the fish stock or
water in a bowl, mix with 3 tbsp of olive oil and
pour over the prawns. Place the prawns in the
marinade covered with foil in the refrigerator
for approximately 2 hours.
Remove the prawns from the marinade,
heat the rest of the olive oil in a pan and sauté
the prawns on each side for approximately
2 minutes.
Towards the end of the cooking, pour the rest
of the marinade over the prawns, mix and add
the water or fish stock.
Arrange on plates and serve with freshly baked
baguettes or steamed rice.

**Sautéed prawns with tomato
and rosemary**

20 prawns, fresh and with head

4 plum tomatoes, peeled, seeds removed,
and cubed

1 small garlic clove, finely chopped

1 sprig of thyme
1 sprig of rosemary

Pinch chopped fennel seeds

5 tbsp extra virgin olive oil

Sea salt
Freshly ground black pepper

50 ml / 1 ½ fl oz / ¼ cup water or fish stock

Wash the prawns and let them dry on paper towels.
Place them in a ceramic bowl.
Put all the ingredients except for the fish stock
or water in a bowl, mix with 3 tbsp of olive oil and
pour over the prawns. Place the prawns in the
marinade covered with foil in the refrigerator for
approximately 2 hours.
Remove the prawns from the marinade, heat the
rest of the olive oil in a pan and sauté the prawns on
each side for approximately 2 minutes. Towards the
end of the cooking, pour the rest of the marinade
over the prawns, mix and add the water or fish stock.
Arrange on plates and serve with freshly baked
baguettes or steamed rice.

TIP
A pan full of sautéed prawns in the middle of a
kitchen table, a fresh baguette and a light white wine
is wonderful for any party, and is particularly easy to
prepare so the host does not have to be permanently
in the kitchen.
Do not fear the garlic because if everyone eats
it none of your friends can complain.

Three ways to prepare prawns

**Sautéed prawns with lemongrass
and ginger**

20 prawns, fresh and with head

1 small garlic clove, finely chopped

1 fresh stalk lemon grass, sliced in rings

1 thumbs width piece of ginger, peeled
and finely grated

½ tsp curry powder

2 tbsp soy sauce
5 tbsp peanut oil

Sea salt
Freshly ground black pepper

50 ml / 1 ½ fl oz / ¼ cup water or fish stock

Prawns should marinate for at least 2 hours in the marinade
so the herbs and spices can release their aroma.

Wash the prawns and let them dry on paper towels.
Place them in a ceramic bowl. Put all the ingredients
except for the fish stock or water in a bowl, mix with
3 tbsp of peanut oil and pour over the prawns.
Place the prawns in marinade covered with foil
in the refrigerator for approximately 2 hours.
Remove the prawns from the marinade, heat the rest
of the peanut oil in a pan and sauté the prawns on
each side for approximately 2 minutes.
Towards the end of the cooking, pour the rest of the
marinade over the prawns, mix and add the water or
fish stock. Arrange on plates and serve with basmati
rice or Asian noodles.

Rouille

1 floury potato, peeled

5 garlic cloves, peeled

Several saffron threads
½ tsp paprika
Sea salt

150 ml / 5 fl oz / ¾ cup water or fish stock

2 egg yolks

150 ml / 5 fl oz / ¾ cup olive oil

Cut the potatoes into pieces and the garlic into
slices. Heat 1 tbsp olive oil, add the potato,
garlic slices, saffron and salt to taste (1).
Heat gently and dust with paprika (2 and 3).
Add the liquid and cook the potato until soft
(4). Remove the pot from the stove and finely
mash the potato with a fork and then let it
cool. Using a whisk, blend in the egg
yolks and then the olive oil, drop
by drop. Stir until well mixed.
Season with sea salt to taste.

*25

Fish stock

Sea urchin sauce

Cream of shellfish soup

Stocks and sauces

Crayfish stock

White wine fish sauce

Small monkfish on a bed of stewed pepper and onion with rosemary

*45

4 monkfish skinned and
cleaned, 300 g / 10 ½ oz each

2 green peppers
1 red pepper

1 white onion, peeled
1 red onion, peeled

3 potatoes, peeled

10 garlic cloves, unpeeled

5 sprigs of thyme
2 sprigs of rosemary

8 tbsp extra virgin olive oil

100 ml / 3 ¼ fl oz / ½ cup fish or vegetable stock

Sea salt

Freshly ground black pepper

Halve the peppers lengthwise and remove the
stem and seeds. Depending on their size, cut
each half lengthwise in 4 cm (2 in) thick pieces.
Quarter the onions and also cut in 4 cm (2 in)
thick pieces. Cut the peeled potatoes in 2 cm
(1 in) thick segments and set aside in water.
Heat half the olive oil in a large pan. Dab the
fish dry with a paper towel, season with salt and
pepper and place it backside down in the hot
pan and sauté. After 3 minutes turn the fish and
sauté the other side for 2 minutes. Remove and
set aside. In the same pan sauté and season the
vegetables. Place the vegetables into a rectangular
casserole dish. Drain the potatoes and let them
dry on paper towels. In the same pan add the
rest of the olive oil and sauté the potato pieces
together with the garlic cloves, skin still on,
for about 5 minutes stirring occasionally.
Add to the vegetables and place the fish on top.

Lay the thyme and rosemary sprigs on the fish
and add the fish stock.
Place in a preheated 220° C oven and bake
for approximately 20 minutes, basting regularly
with the juices from the pan.
Monkfish is ready when the skin on the end of
the tail begins to loosen. Place on plates with
the stewed vegetables and juice from the pan.

TIP
Vegetables may vary. It is only important
that they are fresh and aromatic. Try also
artichokes, aubergines and tomatoes. The
potatoes are the best part in this dish as they
fully absorb the fish broth and aromas.

Baste the monkfish with the juices now and then to keep the fillets from drying out.

Sautéed shrimp on avocado salad with pomegranate seeds

A small trick to remove the vein: stick a toothpick in the centre top of the back and lift it out.

20 fresh shrimps, with head and shell

2 tbsp extra virgin olive oil

2 ripe avocados

1 pomegranate, seeds removed

3 tbsp sunflower oil
3 tbsp walnut oil

5 tbsp light sherry vinegar

1 tbsp powdered icing sugar

Sea salt
Freshly ground black pepper

Chervil leaves to garnish

Twist the heads off the shrimps and peel off the shells of the tails except for the tip. Remove the vein from the back with a toothpick. Heat the olive oil in a non-stick pan, add the shrimp and season with sea salt and black pepper.
Sauté on both sides for approximately 2 minutes and set the pan aside.
Peel and halve the avocados, discard the stone, slice and arrange on 4 plates.

For the vinaigrette combine the sherry vinegar, powdered sugar, sea salt and black pepper. Slowly add the sunflower and walnut oils and mix with a whisk. Add the pomegranate seeds to the dressing and pour over the avocado slices. Arrange the shrimp on top and garnish with chervil leaves.

*20

Grouper

Great weever

Cockles

Monkfish

Brill

Red mullet

Catfish

Prawns

Red snapper

Octopus

Swordfish

Swimming crab

Sardines

St. Petersfish

31

1 European lobster
2 Razor clam
3 Crayfish
4 Red scorpion fish
5 Squid
6 Dublin Bay prawn
7 Hake
8 Sole
9 Skate
10 Turbot
11 European crayfish
12 Tuna fillet

Shrimp

RUSSIAN
CAVIAR
MALOSSOL
CASPIAN CAVIAR BALYKCORPORATION KASPRYBA
ASTRAKHAN

Cod

Caviar

White shrimp

African rock lobster

Whelk

Gurnard

Whitebait

Sea urchin

Small crayfish

Salmon

Cuttlefish

Sea bream

Mussels

Rainbow trout

Sautéed Dublin Bay
prawns in parsley butter

20 fresh Dublin Bay prawns

100 g / 3 ½ oz butter

1 garlic clove, finely chopped
1 shallot, peeled and finely chopped

1 bunch of parsley, finely chopped

Juice of 1 lemon

Sea salt
Pinch of cayenne pepper

1 lemon, quartered

Wash the Dublin Bay prawns, leave whole and dab dry
with paper towels. Melt the butter in a large pan and
lay the prawns in side-by-side and sauté on both sides
for approximately 2 minutes. Add the chopped garlic
and the shallot, stirring until transparent.
Sprinkle with the chopped parsley, douse with the
lemon juice and season with the cayenne pepper.
Place on plates and serve with a lemon quarter.

TIP
A typical summer meal with bread for dipping in the
herb butter. Serve with chilled white wine.

Fried sardines with olives

400 g / 14 oz small sardines

100 g / 3 ½ oz instant flour

80 g / 3 oz green olives

1 lemon, quartered

2 litres / 64 fl oz / 8 cups peanut oil for frying

Coarse sea salt

Under running water pinch off the heads of the sardines and wash them well. Lay on paper towels to dry. Place the dry sardines in a large sieve and sprinkle with flour. Shake the sieve a bit to remove the excess flour and place immediately in the 160° C hot peanut oil and fry for 2 minutes. Place on paper towels and sprinkle with sea salt. Arrange on small plates with the olives and garnish with lemon quarters.

TIP
This type of sardine is often served in the Mediterranean with an apéritif.
Since the sardines are so small they can be eaten whole without any worry.

They taste best with almost nothing at all. Before frying the sardines remove the heads and rinse well. Cover with flour and shake off the excess. They should only be lightly dusted with the flour.

*15

Three ways
to prepare tuna

Three ways to prepare tuna

Tuna tartare with cilantro

400 g / 14 oz raw tuna fillet
2 tbsp light soy sauce
1 tbsp sesame oil
1 tbsp coriander, coarsely chopped
1 lime

Cut the tuna fillet into small cubes. Mix the tuna in
a bowl with the sesame oil, soy sauce and chopped
coriander. Quarter and add the lime.
Squeeze on the lime juice while serving, as the acidic
juice will change the color of the fish to a somewhat
unattractive white.

Tuna belly is a delicacy and highly appreciated, especially in Japan, for its fatty consistency.

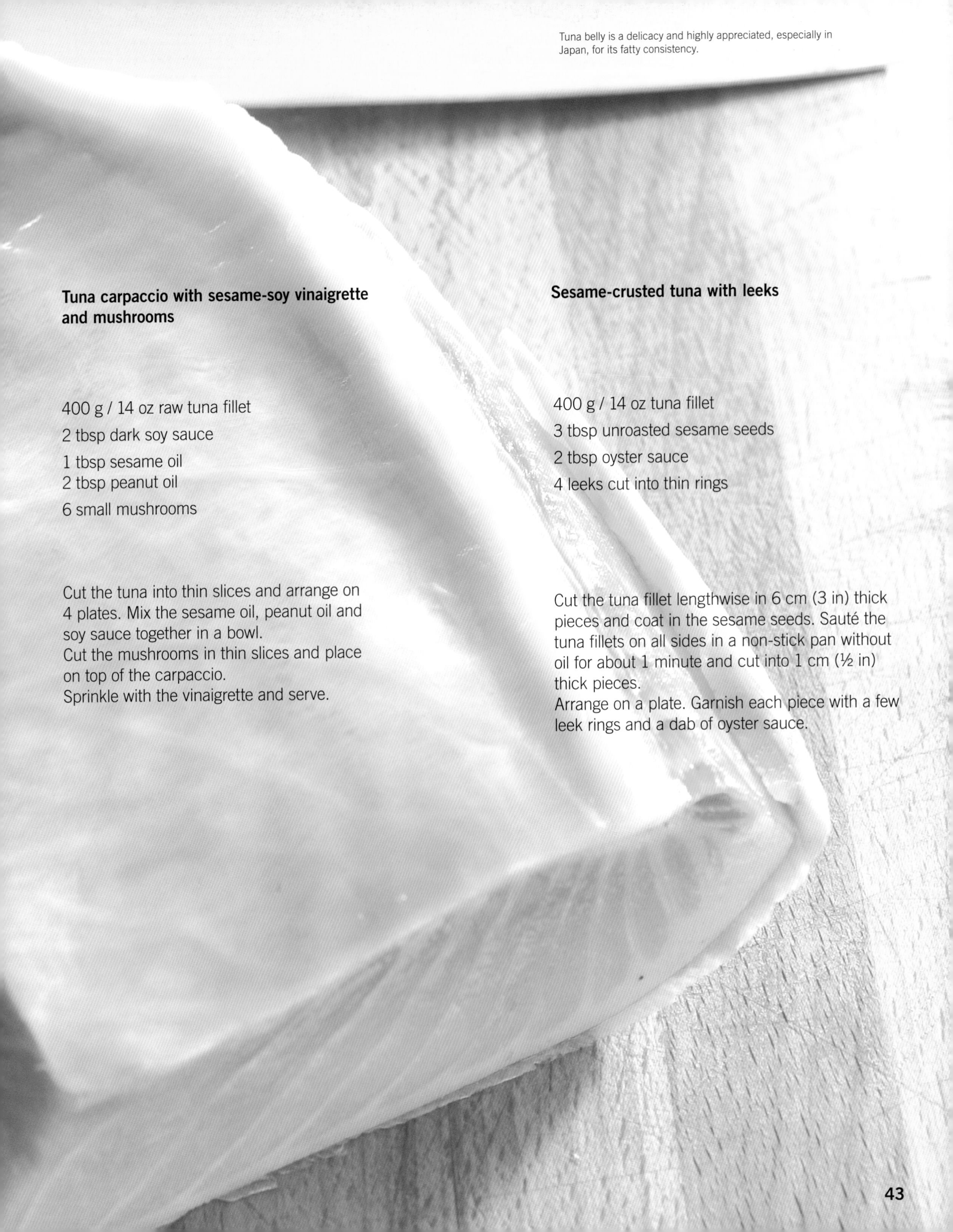

Tuna carpaccio with sesame-soy vinaigrette and mushrooms

400 g / 14 oz raw tuna fillet
2 tbsp dark soy sauce
1 tbsp sesame oil
2 tbsp peanut oil
6 small mushrooms

Cut the tuna into thin slices and arrange on 4 plates. Mix the sesame oil, peanut oil and soy sauce together in a bowl.
Cut the mushrooms in thin slices and place on top of the carpaccio.
Sprinkle with the vinaigrette and serve.

Sesame-crusted tuna with leeks

400 g / 14 oz tuna fillet
3 tbsp unroasted sesame seeds
2 tbsp oyster sauce
4 leeks cut into thin rings

Cut the tuna fillet lengthwise in 6 cm (3 in) thick pieces and coat in the sesame seeds. Sauté the tuna fillets on all sides in a non-stick pan without oil for about 1 minute and cut into 1 cm (½ in) thick pieces.
Arrange on a plate. Garnish each piece with a few leek rings and a dab of oyster sauce.

Mussels à la Provençal

1 ½ kg / approx. 3 lbs cleaned mussels

4 tbsp extra virgin olive oil

2 shallots, finely chopped
2 garlic cloves, finely chopped

8 plum tomatoes, peeled, quartered and cubed

2 bay leaves
1 sprig of thyme

200 ml / 6 ½ fl oz / ¾ cup tomato juice

Sea salt
½ tsp brown sugar
Freshly ground black pepper

½ bunch of basil

For this dish it is best to use sun-ripened plum tomatoes.

Wash the mussels well and check again if all
of them are really fresh. Then put them on
a rack to drain.
Heat the olive oil in a large pot and lightly cook
the shallots and garlic. Put in the tomato cubes
and season with the brown sugar, sea salt and
black pepper. Add the thyme and bay leaves
and allow the tomato cubes to soften.
Add the tomato juice and then the mussels to
the sauce, cover and quickly bring to the boil.
Cook for 5-10 minutes, stirring occasionally, until
all the mussels open. Just before they are done,
stir in the basil that has been cut into strips.
Serve from the pot or in a bowl.

TIP
With the tomatoes, add a sliced courgette, bell
pepper and aubergine to the tomato sauce. This
way you have a wonderful mussel stew which you
can also vary with other provençal vegetables.
Mussels in fresh vegetables à la Provençal: what
more could one want?

Mussels with vegetables
in white wine sauce

1 ½ kg / approx. 3 lbs cleaned mussels

30 g / 1 oz butter

1 shallot, finely chopped
1 garlic clove, finely chopped

2 peeled carrots cut into thin strips
1 leek, cut into strips
2 celery stalks, cut into strips

250 ml / 8 fl oz / 1 cup dry white wine

200 ml / 6 ½ fl oz / ¾ cup cream

½ bunch of parsley, finely chopped

Sea salt
Freshly ground white pepper

In this recipe the vegetables and the white wine make for a milder variation for the mussels.

Wash the mussels well and check again if all of them are really fresh. Then put them on a rack to drain.
Melt and froth the butter in a large pot, then add the shallot and garlic and let it cook for several minutes. Add the vegetable strips, salt and pepper, cooking until softened.
Add the mussels and the white wine and cover immediately with a lid. Quickly bring to the boil. Stir occasionally as the mussels open.
Take the opened mussels out of the pot with a slotted spoon and put them in a bowl. Cover the bowl with aluminium foil.

Reduce the broth down to half and add the cream. Bring to the boil again briefly, mix in the parsley and if necessary season with sea salt and white pepper. Pour the sauce over mussels and serve immediately.

Toro with wasabi

300 g / 10 oz toro (fatty tuna belly)
5 fresh spring onions
1 small bottle light soy sauce
1 tbsp wasabi powder – green Japanese horseradish
1 tbsp water

Remove the skin from the fish, as well as any remaining
sinuous parts, using a very sharp knife. Depending
on the size, cut lengthwise once or twice and then
cut into thin 6 cm (3 in) long strips.
Arrange on a wooden board.
Wash and cut the spring onions into thin rings. Mix the
wasabi powder with water. Pour the light soy sauce into
a small bowl and add the wasabi to it.
Dip the pieces of toro in the sauce and eat it with the
spring onions. Serve with Japanese beer.

*15

Small potatoes with sour cream and caviar

300 g / 10 oz small floury potatoes

100 g / 3 ½ oz caviar, of your preferred type

200 g / 7 oz / 1 cup sour cream

Sea salt

Peel the potatoes and cut them in half lengthwise. Cut off one end so the potatoes do not tip over. Boil them in salt water and then drain.
Arrange the potatoes on a platter. Put a bit of sour cream on each warm potato half and then add the caviar using a mother of pearl spoon.

TIP
To truly enjoy the caviar, cook fewer potatoes and instead cover each potato half with an abundance of caviar. The other option is to buy more caviar. Do not bother with unnecessary accompaniments like onions, lemon and chopped egg.
Good caviar is recognizable by its firm consistency, that it is not too liquidy in the middle and by its wonderful soft and nutty flavour.

Caviar – a delicacy which not only tastes good
in the classic manner with sour cream and blinis
but also can beautifully crown numerous dishes.

Baked razor clams with garlic and soy sauce

1 kg / approx. 2 lbs fresh razor clams

8 tbsp extra virgin olive oil

3 garlic cloves, finely chopped

1 bunch of flat-leaf parsley, chopped

4 tbsp soy sauce

4 tbsp breadcrumbs

Wash the razor clams under running water, cut them open with a sharp knife, and place them opened end up on a baking sheet. Combine the chopped garlic, parsley, olive oil, and soy sauce and drip it over the opened clams with a spoon. Sprinkle them with breadcrumbs and bake for 5 minutes in a 230° C oven.

Due to the size of the clams the baking goes very quickly. When the breadcrumbs are golden they are ready.

Open the washed razor clams with a sharp knife, lay them close to each other on a tray and add the marinade.

*20

Swordfish with green olives, dried tomatoes and water cress

4 swordfish steaks 250 g / 9 oz each

4 tbsp extra virgin olive oil

12 garlic cloves, unpeeled

1 tsp thin strips of lemon rind

20 g / ¾ oz butter

100 g / 3 ½ oz small mushrooms, halved

100 g / 3 ½ oz green olives with stones
60 g / 2 oz marinated dried tomatoes

150 ml / 5 fl oz / ¾ cup dry white wine

1 bunch of water cress

Sea salt
Freshly ground black pepper
Lemon wedges to garnish

Wash the swordfish and dab dry with a paper towel. Heat half the olive oil in a large pan with the slightly crushed garlic cloves still in their skins. Cook lightly and then set aside. Put the swordfish which has been seasoned with the salt and pepper in the pan. Add the lemon peel to give the fish a nice fresh taste. Turn the pieces of fish after 3 minutes and sauté on the other side. Take the fish out and cover it with foil to keep it warm. Put the butter in the pan and sauté the halved mushrooms.
Add the olives and coarsely chopped dried tomatoes and splash with the white wine. Let it all simmer for a minute.
Meanwhile, wash the water cress. Dress with a bit of lemon juice and the rest of the olive oil.

Place the salad on one side of the plate, and on the other, the swordfish with the olive-tomato sauce on top.
Garnish with the lemon wedges and serve with white bread.

TIP
Tuna also tastes very good prepared in this manner.

*40

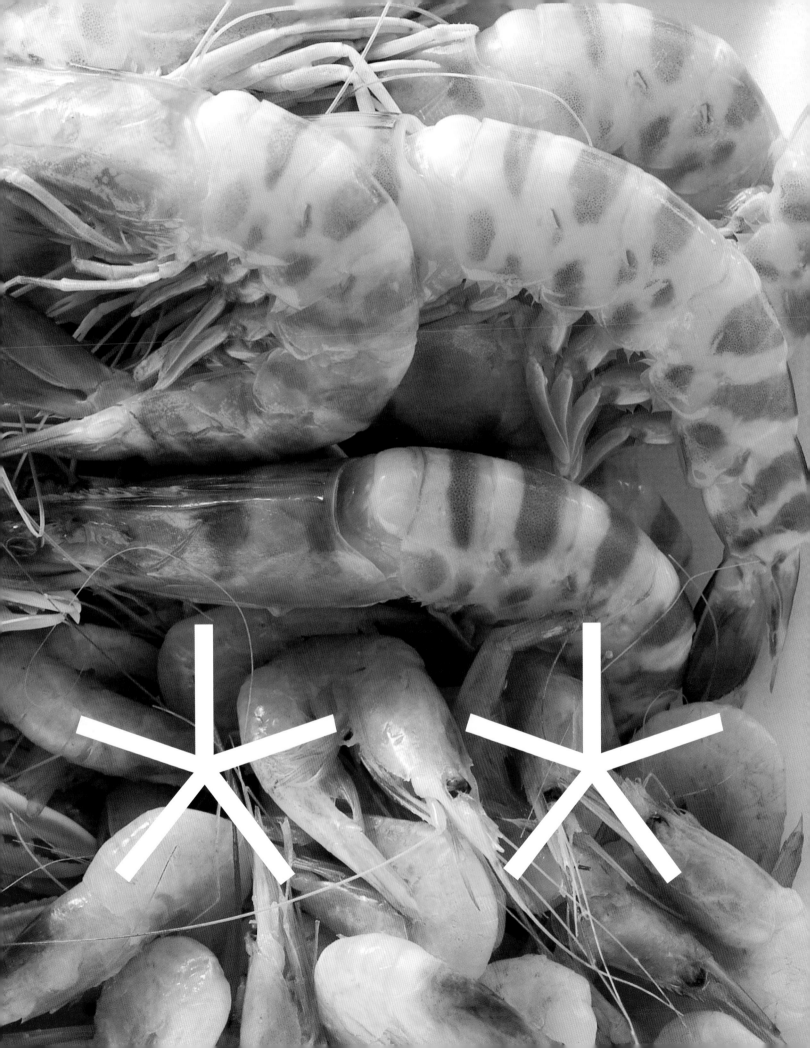

Crayfish stock

Ingredients for 2 litres

2 kg / 4 lbs 6 oz shells and claws
of crayfish and prawns

60 ml / 2 fl oz / ¼ cup olive oil
100 g / 3 ½ oz butter

3 garlic cloves, halved

2 sprigs of thyme

2 carrots, peeled

1 fennel bulb
3 celery stalks
3 shallots, peeled
1 white onion, peeled

1 tsp tomato paste
4 tbsp ketchup

2 bay leaves
½ tsp lightly ground white
peppercorns
3 cloves

A few parsley stems

50 ml / 1 ½ fl oz / ¼ cup cognac
250 ml / 8 fl oz / 1 ¼ cups white wine
50 ml / 1 ½ fl oz / ¼ cup white port

2 ½ litres / 82 fl oz of water or fish stock

Sea salt

Basis for any stock: chopped vegetables, herbs
and salt.
Cut the crayfish into small pieces with scissors.
Also cut the claws in two.
Adds to the taste: the shells of the crayfish (1-4).

TIP
Only use very fresh crayfish for the stock. Should the
shells already have black spots the stock could become
too dark and have a bitter taste.

Crayfish stock

Cut the crayfish and shrimp shells into small pieces with scissors. Crush the crayfish claws into small pieces either with the kitchen scissors or the back of a heavy knife and slowly sauté them in a wide pot in the olive oil and butter. Constantly stir the shells (5), not allowing them to get too dark. Add the garlic cloves (6) and the cut thyme sprigs. Cook a bit longer.

Meanwhile, cut the vegetables in 1 cm (½ in) cubes and add them with the bay leaves and spices (7).

Continue frying until the vegetables are soft. Set the pot of shells away from the heat and add the tomato paste and ketchup. Let cook for a minute. Cooking the tomato paste reduces its acidity. Add the parsley stems, stir and add the cognac (8).

Then add the port and white wine and let simmer (9).

Add the water or fish stock and simmer for another 15 minutes (10). Pour the broth through a sieve and press out the crayfish shells (11).

Crayfish stock serves as a basis for cream of shellfish soups, seafood pasta dishes or shellfish risotto.

8

9

** 60

Sautéed skate wing
à la Grenoble with boiled potatoes

4 small skate, skinned, 350 g / 12 ½ oz each

4 tbsp sunflower oil
80 g / 3 oz butter

500 g / 18 oz floury potatoes

1 tbsp coarse Meaux mustard

Lemon twists

1 tbsp capers

1 tbsp flat-leaf parsley, cut into fine strips

Sea salt

Skate is a very sensitive fish.
It should be covered in cling film
and kept cool until preparing.

Wash the skate and pat with paper towels.
Salt and place in one large or two medium-sized
non-stick pans, thicker side down first. Cook for
about 5 minutes on medium heat, adding the
sunflower oil and then turn. Remove the oil with
a spoon and add the butter.
Slowly sauté for a further 5 minutes and
continually baste with the frothy butter.
Meanwhile, cut the peeled potatoes into wide
lengthwise pieces and boil them in salt water.
Drain and let them steam a bit. This way they
absorb the butter better.
Spread the mustard on the skate, add the
capers and lemon twists and sprinkle with
parsley. Spoon the butter over the garnish
several more times and arrange on plates.
Place the potatoes beside the fish and serve.

TIP
The best tasting capers are Nonpareil's
capers. They are the very small and aromatic
buds of the caper bush.

Rustic puréed fish soup with saffron and basil

500 g / 18 oz red mullet

500 g / 18 oz great weever

8 tbsp extra virgin olive oil

3 garlic cloves, peeled

½ tsp saffron threads
3 sprigs of thyme

1 red pepper
1 yellow pepper

2 carrots, peeled

1 fennel bulb
2 celery stalks
1 white onion

2 sprigs of thyme
3 bay leaves
½ tsp crushed fennel seeds
½ tsp crushed black peppercorns
½ tsp saffron threads

50 ml / 1 ½ fl oz / ¼ cup Pastis
250 ml / 8 fl oz / 1 ¼ cups robust white wine
2 litres / 64 fl oz / 8 cups water

½ bunch of basil

Sea salt
Finely ground black pepper

Basil leaves to garnish

Remove the scales and clean the fish well. Cut out the gills with kitchen scissors. Cut the fish, including the heads, into about 5 cm (2 in) pieces. Marinate them in sliced garlic, half the olive oil, saffron threads and thyme sprigs for about an hour.
Cut the peppers in half and remove the stem, seeds and white parts and then wash them. Cut the pepper, carrots, fennel and onion in 1 cm (½ in) cubes and

sauté in the rest of the olive oil in a wide pot. Add and roast the coarsely cut bay leaves as well as the peppercorns and fennel seeds so that the spices can release their flavours (1). Add the marinated fish (2) and sauté with sea salt (3). Douse first with the Pastis and then with the white wine (4) and let simmer. Coarsely chop and then add the bunch of basil (5). Pour in the cold water and let simmer for approximately 10 minutes (6). Put the entire mixture through the blender and season with sea salt, Pastis and the freshly ground pepper.
Serve in soup bowls and garnish with basil leaves.

TIP
Garlic croutons made from whole wheat bread give the soup a hearty taste.

Cockles in beer sauce and red wine onions

1 ½ kg / approx. 3 lbs cockles

30 g / 1 oz butter

330 ml / 10 fl oz / 1 ¼ cups hot beer

1 sprig of thyme
1 bay leaf

250 ml / 8 fl oz / 1 cup light cream

2 red onions, peeled

1 tbsp sunflower oil

1 tsp brown sugar

Sea salt
Freshly ground black pepper

500 ml / 16 fl oz / 2 cups heavy red wine

A sign of freshness in the cockles is that they open and close. To check, tap the slightly opened ones on the table. Discard the ones which do not close. However, after cooking, discard all those which do not open.

Cut the onions in half and then slice them lengthwise. Sauté in oil, then season with the sugar, sea salt and black pepper and fry until transparent. Simmer in the red wine until it has reduced and the onions have become dark red.
Wash the cockles and let them dry on a rack. Melt the butter in a large casserole dish and let the thyme sprig and bay leaf roast in it for a minute before adding the drained cockles. Add the beer and cover with a lid. Cook until the cockles open. Remove them with a slotted spoon and place in a bowl. Allow the cockle and beer broth to reduce. Add the cream and season with black pepper and sea salt if necessary. Then return the cockles to the dish mixing them in the broth. Arrange on warmed plates and spoon the red wine and onions on top. Serve.

TIP
Best served with the same beer that you also used in cooking.

Lemongrass red snapper with broccoli and ginger

4 fillets of red snapper with skin

4 stalks of lemongrass

2 tbsp Thai fish sauce

2 green chilli

500 g / approx. 1lb broccoli
1 leek cut in rings

4 tbsp oyster sauce

1 tbsp fresh grated ginger

4 tbsp peanut oil

Sea salt

Check the fish fillets with fingers for any possible bones and remove them. Wash the fillets and dab dry with a paper towel. Slit the skin with a sharp knife or razor blade at 3 cm (1 ¼ in) intervals. Cut lemon grass to 13 cm (5 in) and then in quarters lengthwise. Stick four pieces of lemon grass through each of the red snapper fillets and marinate in the fish sauce and sliced chilli. Wash the broccoli and cut the stem into pieces. Slowly sauté the broccoli florets in a pan or wok with half the peanut oil. Add the leek slices and then the oyster sauce. Fold in the grated ginger.
In the meantime, heat a non-stick pan with the rest of the peanut oil and put in the fish fillets skin side down. Sauté for 5 minutes on medium heat and then turn. Arrange the broccoli and leek on warmed plates and place a red snapper fillet on each.
Garnish with the rest of the chilli rings from the pan.

✳✳25

Coconut-coated octopus kebabs on spicy tomato onion sauce

1 fresh octopus, 1 kg / approx. 2 lb

2 garlic cloves, unpeeled

2 sprigs of thyme

1 tbsp white pepper corns
Coarse sea salt

¼ lemon

1 egg white, slightly beaten

100 g / 3 ½ oz coconut flakes

3 tbsp sunflower oil

2 white onions, peeled
1 small garlic clove, finely chopped

2 tbsp sunflower oil

1 tbsp brown sugar

1 tsp tomato paste
1 tbsp sweet and sour chilli sauce
250 ml / 8 fl oz / 1 cup tomato juice

Juice of 2 limes

Sea salt
Freshly ground black pepper

Lime slice to garnish

Wash the octopus under running water and clean it out well.
Boil water in a large pot and season with the sea salt, thyme, garlic cloves in their skin, black pepper and ¼ lemon. Place the octopus in the boiling water and boil for approximately 2 ½ hours.

Rinse the octopus under running water until it is no longer slimy. Then put it in the pot with the seasoning and cook until done.

Coconut-coated octopus kebabs on spicy tomato onion sauce

In the meantime, halve the white onions lengthwise and slice.

Fry the onions in the sunflower oil with the brown sugar, sea salt and freshly ground black pepper until they soften. Do not roast the onions. Add the tomato paste and the chilli sauce and cook a bit longer. Then add the tomato juice and the lime juice and gently simmer for about 10 minutes until the sauce has a chutney-like consistency.

Use a long-pronged fork to check if the octopus is done. Take it from the pot and leave it to cool, cut off the tentacles and remove any dark skin. Cut into 2 cm and 5 cm (1 in and 2 in) pieces and alternately stick one large and one small piece onto wooden skewers.

Dip in beaten egg white and roll in the coconut flakes. Heat oil in a non-stick pan and fry the kebabs on both sides until golden brown.

Put the sauce on the plates and the kebabs on top and garnish with the lime slices.

Marinated octopus and white bean salad

1 fresh octopus, 1 kg / approx. 1lb

2 garlic cloves, unpeeled

2 sprigs of thyme
1 tsp white pepper corns
Coarse sea salt

¼ lemon
Juice of 1 lemon

4 tbsp quality olive oil

200 g / 7 oz small white beans, dried

6 tbsp extra virgin olive oil

1 litre / 32 fl oz liquid or vegetable stock

1 sprig of rosemary

2 garlic cloves, unpeeled

½ bunch of parsley

2 tbsp white wine vinegar

Freshly ground black pepper

1 romaine lettuce, heart only
2 spring onions

The white beans should be marinaded in the oil and finely chopped garlic. The sliced octopus tentacles should be marinaded in a mixture of olive oil and lemon juice.

Wash the octopus under running water and clean it out well.
Boil water in a large pot and season with the sea salt, thyme, garlic cloves in their skin, black pepper and ¼ lemon. Place the octopus in the boiling water and boil for approximately 2 ½ hours.
In the meantime, heat 1 tbsp olive oil in a mid-sized casserole dish and lightly roast a partially crushed unpeeled garlic clove and the rosemary sprig. Add the white beans and the liquid. Let it simmer slowly for approximately 1 hour and if needed add more liquid. Strain the beans in a sieve and put them in a bowl.

Marinate the beans in the white wine vinegar, the rest of the olive oil and finely chopped parsley and garlic. Set aside.
Use a long-pronged fork to check if the octopus is done. Take it from the pot and leave to cool, cut off the tentacles and remove any dark skin. Cut into 3 cm (1 ½ in) pieces and marinate in the lemon juice, olive oil, and some sea salt.
Arrange the washed romaine heart leaves on plates and then the marinated beans and octopus. Sprinkle with rings of spring onion.

TIP
Serve with fresh white bread or grissini.

**180

Deep-fried brill with french fries / fish and chips

There is nothing better than homemade French fries from floury potatoes.

Mixing some oil into the batter will make it crispy.

Frying the French fries twice makes them done on the inside and crunchy.

600 g / 21 oz brill fillets

Juice of 1 lemon

Sea salt
Freshly ground white pepper

2 tbsp flour

500 g / 18 oz floury potatoes

2 litres / 64 fl oz / 8 cups peanut oil

A dash of white wine vinegar

300 g / 10 ½ oz flour
1 tsp baking powder

360 ml / 12 fl oz / 1 ½ cups beer

3 egg yolks
8 tbsp oil
3 egg whites

Salt

Peel the potatoes and cut off the rounded ends so that the same-length French fries can be cut. Cut the potatoes in 1 cm (½ in) thick and 6 cm (3 in) long pieces. Lay them in cold water to soak for about a half an hour. This way the excess starch will be rinsed away and the French fries will be crisper. Put on paper towels and lightly rub dry.

Combine the flour, baking powder, beer and egg yolk in a bowl and whisk into a smooth batter. Mix in the oil bit by bit and let the batter sit for 10-15 minutes. Lightly beat the egg white with some sea salt and carefully fold it into the beer batter. Cut the brill fillets in 3 cm (1 ½ in) and 10 cm (4 in) pieces. Add salt and pepper and mix with the lemon juice. Dust with 2 tbsp flour and dunk in the beer batter. Cover with batter and fry for approximately 5 minutes until golden brown in the preheated 160° C peanut oil.

Use a tall pot to avoid oil spatters in the kitchen. Put the fried fish fillets on a rack on a baking sheet and keep warm in a 100° C preheated oven. Pour the hot oil through a sieve into a tall pot and preheat to 160° C. Put the dried pieces of potato in the hot oil and fry for about 2 minutes without letting them become too brown. Take out and let them dry on paper towels. In the meantime, preheat the oil to 190° C and put in the pre-cooked potatoes. Let them turn golden brown and crisp, remove and leave in a sieve on paper towels to dry. Mix in salt. Arrange the French fries together with the fish and sprinkle with a few drops of white wine vinegar.

TIP
Cod, seafood or peeled shrimp can also be used. Aioli tastes good with this dish. Just don't count the calories!

Filleting a brill

Cut along either side of the spine with a sharp knife
and loosen the fillets from the bones towards the fins (1).
Use the knife to remove the skin (2). Do not discard the
carcasses, instead use them for fish stock.

1

**15

Cod on a bed of beetroot with warm beans and marinated herbs

600 g / 21 oz cod fillet, skin removed

2 tbsp sunflower oil

8 beetroots with leaves

200 g / 7 oz green beans

Sea salt
Brown sugar
1 tsp cumin

2 tbsp fruit vinegar

For vinaigrette:

10 tbsp sunflower oil

6 tbsp cider vinegar

2 tsp sugar
Sea salt
Freshly ground black pepper
½ tsp chopped cumin

For marinated herbs:

½ bunch of parsley
½ bunch of dill

Sea salt
Freshly ground black pepper

1 tbsp cold-pressed sunflower oil

Juice of ½ lemon

1 potato, peeled and cut into slices

4 tbsp sunflower oil

Cook the beetroots until soft in water strongly seasoned with the sea salt, sugar, fruit vinegar and cumin. Beforehand, cut the greens of the beetroot 1 cm (½ in) above the roots. Let cool and then peel. Cut them in half and then again in thin segments.
Cut off the stem end of the beans with a small knife and cook them al dente in salt water.
Run them under cold water and set aside.
To make the vinaigrette combine the cider vinegar with the sugar, sea salt, chopped cumin and pepper and mix in the sunflower oil with a whisk. Pour half on the beetroots and the other half on the beans and let marinate.
Cut the cod into 4 pieces. Heat the oil in a non-stick pan, season the fillets with sea salt and sauté them on both sides.
Tear the parsley and dill into small pieces and combine with sea salt, black pepper, lemon juice and sunflower oil.
Arrange the marinated beetroots in four soup bowls and place a cod fillet on each.
Garnish with the marinated beans and then the mixed herbs. Place the fried thin potato slices on the beetroot slices.

Whole sautéed sole in sage butter with parsley potatoes

4 whole sole 400-500 g / 14-18 oz each

8 tbsp sunflower oil

Juice of 1 lemon

4 tbsp flour

½ bunch of sage

150 g / 5 oz butter

500 g / 1 lb small potatoes

1 bunch of finely chopped parsley

Sea salt

Clean the sole and pull off the skin on both sides starting from the tail fin. Cut out the fin bases and gills with kitchen scissors. Wash and dab dry with a paper towel. Cut along the spine on both sides so that later the fillets are easier to remove. Sprinkle with salt and lemon juice and dust on both sides with flour. Knock off excess flour and sauté golden brown in an oval pan on both sides for 5 minutes. Spoon the oil out of the pan and add 100 g / 3 ½ oz butter and the sage leaves and continue cooking. Continually spoon the frothy butter over the sole and sauté until the sage leaves are crisp.

In the meantime, peel the potatoes and boil them in salt water. Drain and mix with the rest of the butter. Arrange the sole, the parsley and the potatoes on four oval plates and pour the sage butter over.

TIP
Stewed tomatoes or spinach with garlic butter taste wonderful as a side dish to this sole.

Use a large spoon to get the fillets off the bone. This way the fish won't be damaged and the fillet won't fall apart when picked up. Also lift the main fish bone carefully off the fillet underneath with the spoon.

Sauté the sage leaves in the frothy butter until they are crisp. Make sure the butter doesn't turn too brown.

Crispy catfish on red pepper and fennel with saffron sauce

4 catfish fillets, scales scraped and deboned

2 tbsp extra virgin olive oil

2 sprigs of thyme

Sea salt

2 fennel bulbs

1 large red pepper

1 tbsp extra virgin olive oil
40 g / 1 ½ oz butter

1 shallot, finely chopped
1 small clove of garlic, finely diced

½ tsp crushed coriander seeds

Several saffron threads

2 cl / ½ oz Pastis
100 ml / 3 ¼ fl oz / ½ cup dry white wine

150 ml / 5 fl oz / ¾ cup fish or vegetable stock

300 g / 10 oz small peeled potatoes

5 basil leaves
1 tbsp fresh coriander, coarsely chopped
1 tbsp parsley, finely chopped

Wash the catfish fillets and dab dry with a paper towel. Check the fillets with fingertips to make sure there are no more bones, and if necessary remove them. Slit the skin about every 1 cm (½ in) with a very sharp knife or razor blade and set aside.
Cut off the top stem of the fennel bulb, cut the bulb in half and then the halves into small lengthwise segments. Cut the red pepper in half and remove the seeds and white parts and wash. Cut in 2 cm (1 in) thick cubes. Heat the olive oil and half of the butter in a wide casserole dish and sauté the garlic and shallots. Add the crushed coriander seeds and saffron threads and sauté. Mix in the fennel and the pepper and douse with Pastis and white wine and let reduce.

Add the stock, cover and steam for about 8 minutes. In the meantime, boil the small potatoes in salt water, drain and mix with the rest of the butter and the chopped parsley.
Heat the olive oil in a non-stick pan, place the salted catfish fillets skin-side down in the pan and the thyme leaves from the sprig on the fish. Slowly sauté on skin-side only until crisp. This way the fish cooks through slowly from the bottom to the top. Mix the cut strips of basil leaves and chopped coriander leaves into the red pepper and fennel. Arrange the vegetables with their juices and the parsley potatoes on warmed plates. Turn the catfish fillets in the pan and place on the plates with the skin-side up.

Preparing a sea bream

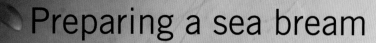

Cut out the fins on the back and behind the head using kitchen scissors.
Cut open the belly and remove the innards (1).
Rinse the cavity out well with cold running water (2).
Turn the sea bream over and cut underneath the head (3).
Thus being able to remove the gills from the bottom of the fish (4).
Rinse well again with running water (5).
Cut off the fins from the belly and tail with scissors (6 and 7).
Scrape off the scales with the help of a knife (8).

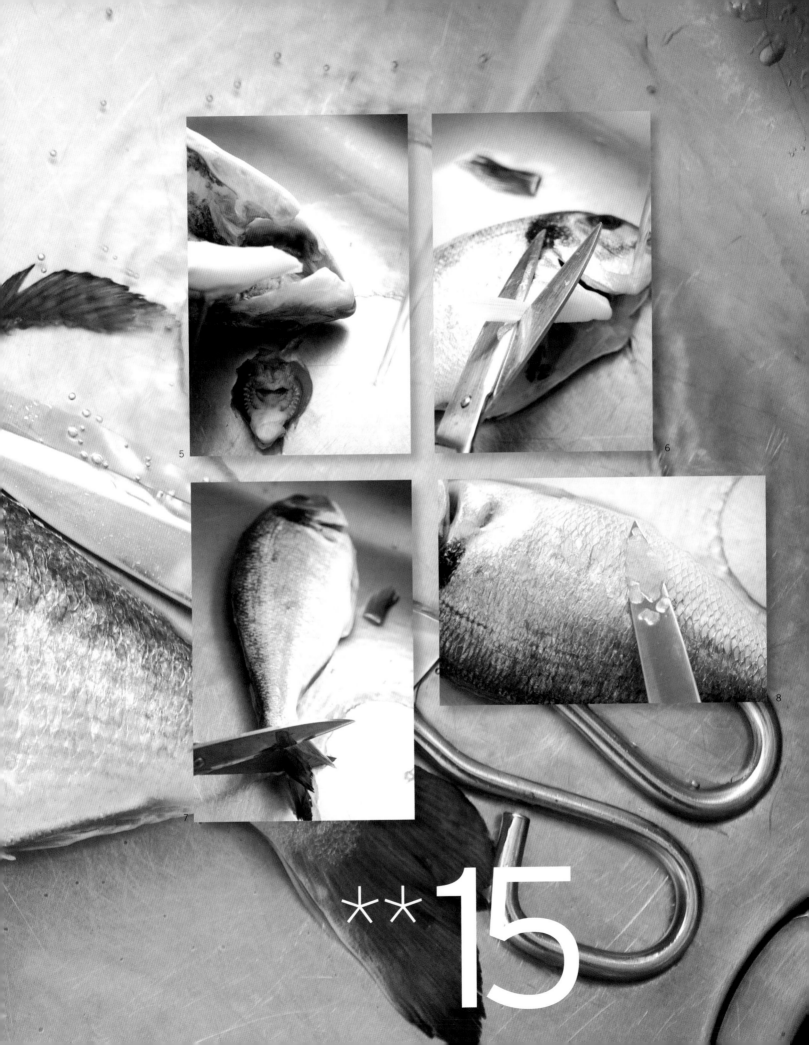

5

6

7

8

**15

Sea bream in three different salt crusts

The coating of salt around the fish should be sealed.
Cooking in this way retains the aroma of the sea bream during the
cooking process which is then released when the salt is removed.

Sea bream in three different salt crusts

4 cleaned sea bream,
not descaled 350-400 g / 12-14 oz

8 lemon slices, with peel

Several parsley sprigs

Pepper salt crust for 4 sea bream

6 kg / 13 lbs coarse unrefined sea salt

4 tbsp each of white, black and red peppercorns

5 egg whites

Put coarse sea salt in a bowl and mix with the whole peppercorns and the egg whites until moist. This allows the salt to bake later into a crust.

Coriander salt crust for 4 sea bream

6 kg / 13 lbs coarse unrefined sea salt

4 tbsp coriander seeds
4 tbsp cumin
1 tbsp cloves

5 egg whites

Put coarse sea salt in a bowl and mix with the whole coriander seeds, the cumin, cloves and the egg whites until moist. This allows the salt to bake later into a crust.

Lemon and fennel leaves salt crust for 4 sea bream

6 kg / 13 lbs coarse unrefined sea salt

2 tbsp fennel seeds
2 tbsp coarsely-ground star anis
1 bunch fennel leaves, dried

Peel of 2 oranges
Peel of 2 lemons

5 egg whites

Put coarse sea salt in a bowl and mix until moist with the egg whites which later allows the salt to bake into a crust. Cut the orange and lemon peel into thin strips and the fennel leaves into 5 cm (2 in) long pieces. Combine with the herbs and the salt.

Mix the salt with the seasoning according to preference: aromatic with coriander seeds, cloves and cumin, fresh and fruity with fennel leaves and lemon and orange peel, or spicy with the three peppers: red, black and white.

Sea bream in three different salt crusts

Preparing the Fish

Clean and pat dry the fish inside and out with a paper towel. Fill each with parsley sprigs and lemon slices to give the fish a fresh taste. Cover a baking tray with aluminium foil. Make a 1 cm (½ in) thick layer of salt on the tray for each fish. Put the fish on the tray and cover with the rest of the salt crust. Press down the salt lightly and put the tray in the 250° C preheated oven. Bake for about half an hour.
The fish is ready when the salt crust begins to brown lightly on the lower edges.
Take out the fish and with a heavy spoon knock the salt crust on the sides and remove the lid. Scratch off the salt on the sides so the fish is easily visible. Skin the fish and with a spoon and a fork carefully lift the fish fillet onto a preheated plate.
The best way to serve this dish is simply to dress the fillets with a few drops of very good olive oil and lemon juice and serve. Fresh parsley potatoes and baby spinach make a pleasant side dish.

Red snapper fillet on a bed of radicchio and frisee with black olive pesto

500 g / approx. 1 lb red snapper without the skin
Juice of ½ lemon
1 tbsp extra virgin olive oil
20 g / ¾ oz butter

3 radicchio
1 small head of frisee lettuce
2 ripe tomatoes

5 tbsp sherry vinegar
1 tbsp powdered icing sugar
½ tsp medium mustard
8 tbsp extra virgin olive oil
Freshly ground black pepper
Basil leaves to garnish

For the tapenade:
100 g / 3 ¼ oz black olives with stones removed
60 ml / 2 fl oz / ¼ cup extra virgin olive oil
40 g / 1 ¼ oz ground almonds

Check the red snapper fillet again to make sure there are no more bones and if necessary remove them. Cut in 2-3 cm (1-1 ½ in) strips. Season with sea salt and freshly-ground black pepper, mix with olive oil and let marinate.
In the meantime, tear the salad into bite-sized pieces, wash and dry in a salad spinner. Blend together the sherry vinegar, powdered sugar, sea salt, black pepper and mustard with a whisk and add the oil bit by bit, stirring continually. Cut the stem out of the tomatoes and cut into pieces.

To make the tapenade, mix the black olives with the olive oil and the ground almonds in a blender until creamy.
Melt butter in a non-stick pan and sauté the marinated red snapper strips for 3 to 5 minutes until golden brown. Dress the salad and tomatoes with the vinaigrette and put on plates. Place the sautéed snapper on top and spread with the tapenade. Garnish with basil leaves and freshly ground black pepper.

Grilled whole catfish with mint

2 catfish 800 g / 28 oz each

1 bunch of mint
1 tsp fennel seeds
1 tsp red peppercorns
3 cloves
2 cloves of garlic, finely chopped
6 tbsp extra virgin olive oil

500 g / 1 lb peeled potatoes
2 tbsp olive oil for sautéing

Sea salt
Freshly ground black pepper

Scrape off the scales of the catfish, clean and cut out the gills with scissors. Cut off the back, belly and side fins and trim the tail fin. Dry inside and out with a paper towel. Slit the skin of the fillets every 3 cm (1 ½ in) going down from the spine to enable the mint marinade to soak in.

Pull off the mint leaves and save some for garnishing. Chop the rest of the leaves finely and put in a bowl. Add 1 tbsp olive oil to the cloves, peppercorns and fennel seeds and chop with a heavy knife. The oil helps prevent the peppercorns and seeds from jumping away. Add the chopped garlic and the rest of the oil to the mint. Spread the marinade on the catfish and especially into the slits. Leave to marinate for ½ an hour at room temperature. Then salt inside and out and place in a preheated ridge-bottomed skillet. Grill on both sides for 10 minutes.
In the meantime, cut the potatoes in half lengthwise and then cut into strips. Boil for 2 minutes, drain and let cool for a few minutes. Heat the olive oil in a non-stick pan and add the potatoes. Season with sea salt and fresh pepper and fry until golden brown. Put them in an oven-proof dish and place the grilled fish in the centre. Finish cooking the fish for 8-10 minutes in a preheated 160° C oven. Garnish with the small mint leaves and serve.

TIP
Substitute basil and rosemary for the mint.

✳✳ 45

Grilled whole catfish with mint

The ingredients for this spicy marinade are fresh herbs and aromatic spices. Chop the spices in some olive oil with a heavy knife. Slit the catfish numerous times so the marinade can soak in. Generously spread the marinade over the fish.

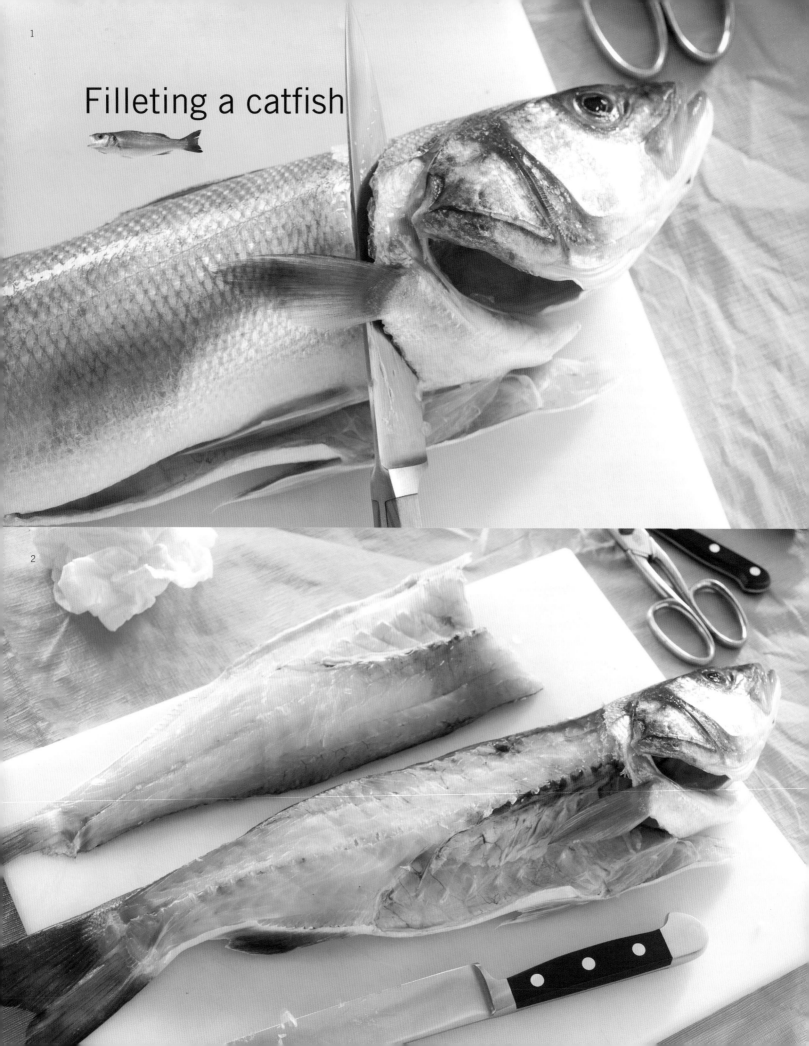

Filleting a catfish

Using a sharp knife cut directly behind the head towards the spine of the fish (1).
Then tip the knife and move it along the spine to the tail fin and remove the fillet (2).
Turn the catfish over and do the same on the other side (3).
Remove the inner bones from the fillets (4).

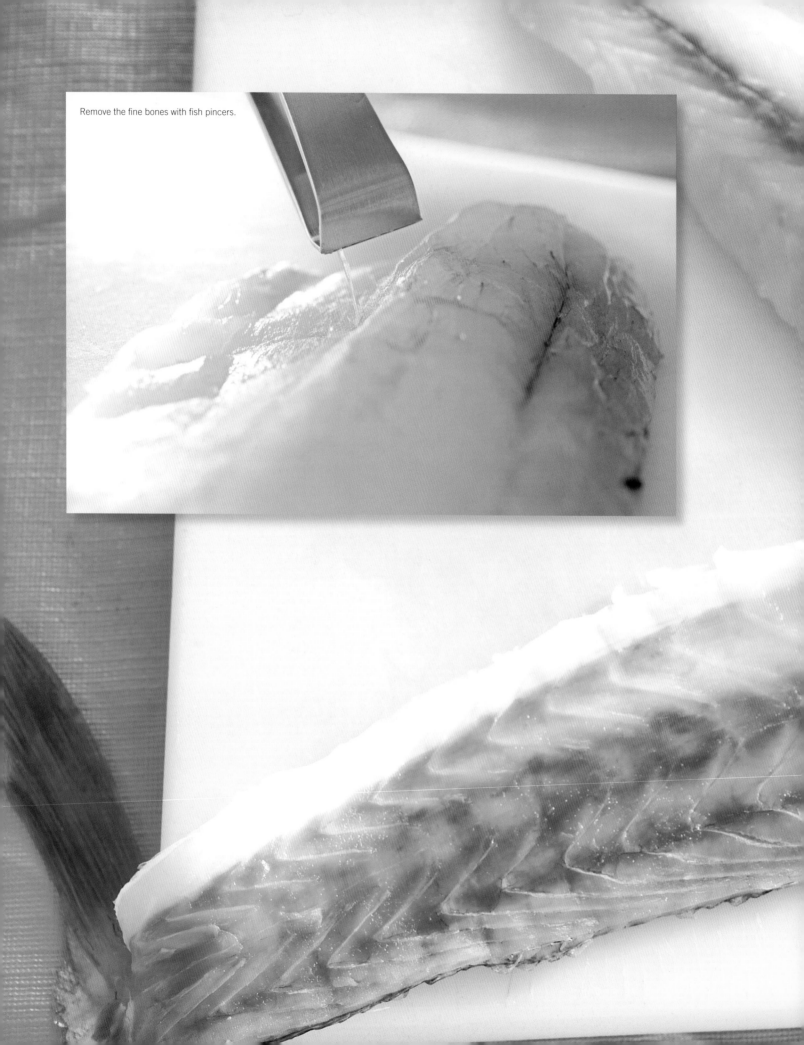

Remove the fine bones with fish pincers.

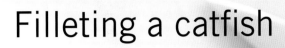

Filleting a catfish

**20

Lay the fillets skin-side down and using a knife pull them off the skin starting at the tail end.

Grilled red scorpion with fennel leaves on a bed of broad beans and garlic

1 red scorpion 1.2 kg / 2 ½ lbs, scaled and cleaned

3 cloves of garlic, unpeeled

A few sprigs of dried fennel leaves

2 cl / 6 ½ fl oz Pastis

3 tbsp extra virgin olive oil

1 bunch of spring onions

20 g / ¾ oz butter

1 kg / 2 lbs 3 oz broad beans

Freshly ground nutmeg
Sea salt
Freshly ground black pepper

Wash the red scorpion inside and out under running water, dry and cut off the head with a sharp knife. Use the head for fish stock or bouillabaisse and set aside. Cut off the back, belly and side fins with kitchen scissors. Cut fish horizontally into four pieces and put in a bowl. Cut the garlic, in its skin, into thin slices and the fennel leaves into 5 cm (2 in) long pieces, combine with the olive oil and Pastis and marinate the fish for 15 minutes at room temperature. Heat a ridge-bottomed skillet and put in the red scorpion with the cut side face down.
Grill on each side for about 8 minutes, repeatedly spooning over the marinade.
Cut off the greens and stems of the spring onions and wash well. Cut in rings and sauté in melted butter until transparent. Boil the beans in generously salted water for about 2 minutes, drain and add to the hot spring onions. Season with the nutmeg, black pepper and sea salt.
Arrange the bean and spring onion mixture on a platter and place the grilled red scorpion on top. Garnish with the roasted garlic and fennel leaves from the marinade.

✳✳60

Serrano-wrapped salmon scaloppine on spinach and sage potatoes

8 salmon fillet strips 80 g / 3 oz each

8 slices Serrano ham

60 g / 2 oz butter

400 g / 14 oz medium-sized potatoes, peeled

3 sage sprigs

4 tbsp extra virgin olive oil

500 g / 1 lb washed spinach

1 clove of garlic, peeled

Freshly ground nutmeg
Sea salt
Freshly ground black pepper

Spanish Serrano ham is stronger than Italian Parma ham, but lends the sautéed salmon a hearty aroma.

Halve and then quarter the potatoes lengthwise. Boil for two minutes, drain and let cool for a few minutes. Heat 4 tbsp of olive oil in a pan and slowly cook the potatoes for another ten minutes on all sides until golden brown and then season with black pepper. When done, mix in the sage leaves.

Wrap each salmon strip in a piece of Serrano ham and sauté in half the butter for about 1 minute on each side.

In the meantime, froth the rest of the butter and add the cleaned and dried spinach. Season with the sea salt and freshly ground nutmeg. Place the garlic clove on a fork and stir the spinach with it to give the spinach its taste.

Arrange the spinach in the centre of the warmed plates, the potatoes around the outside and the scaloppine on top of the spinach. Spoon the juices from the salmon pan over the fish.

Serrano-wrapped salmon scaloppine on spinach and sage potatoes

Cut the salmon in slices and wrap each in a piece of Serrano ham. Salt the salmon scaloppine carefully as the Serrano is already salty.

Saint Petersfish on a bed of lentils and balsamic bacon sauce

600 g / 21 oz skinned Saint Petersfish (dory) fillet

1 tsp orange peel cut in fine strips

20 g / ¾ oz butter
2 tbsp sunflower oil

40 g / 1 ¼ oz smoked bacon, in small pieces (lardons)

20 g / ¾ oz butter

2 shallots, diced
1 clove of garlic, finely chopped

120 g / 4 oz green lentils, soaked

½ tsp tomato paste

250 ml / 8 fl oz / 1 cup fish stock

1 sprig of thyme

200 ml / 7 fl oz / ¾ cup light cream
2 tbsp crème fraîche

Sea salt
Freshly ground black pepper

4 cl / 12 ¾ fl oz balsamic vinegar

Parsley to garnish

Fry the cubes of bacon in hot butter for the sauce. Sauté the diced shallots and the garlic and then do the same with the lentils. Mix in the tomato paste and cook for a moment.
Add the fish stock and the thyme sprig and let simmer for about 20 minutes. Add the cream and mix in the crème fraîche. Season with the sea salt, black pepper and balsamic vinegar.
Cut the Saint Petersfish fillets in medium-sized strips and season with salt.

Heat the butter and oil in a coated pan and put in the fish strips.
Season with sea salt and sprinkle with the orange peel strips. Slowly sauté, continually basting with the oil and butter from the pan. The butter should not burn and the fish should keep its wonderful white colour. Put the lentils onto warmed plates and place the sautéed Saint Petersfish strips on top.

TIP
Serve either small parsley potatoes or freshly cooked basmati rice as a side dish.

Filleting a Saint Petersfish (dory)

Insert a sharp knife directly behind the head and cut along close to the spine in the direction of the tail (1).
Cut the fillet free from the bone along the bottom side also in the direction of the tail (2).
Turn the fish over and remove the other fillet in the same manner.
Cut off the fins with kitchen scissors.
Remove the fillet from the skin using the knife (3).

✷✷20

3

1

2

Dried cod crostini with tomatoes and spring onions

400 g / 14 oz dried cod, preferably from the back of the fish

1 litre / 32 fl oz / 4 cups whole milk

1 dried chilli
3 cloves
½ tsp white peppercorns
2 bay leaves

1 garlic clove unpeeled, lightly crushed

A few saffron threads

1 large floury potato cooked in its skin

6 tbsp extra virgin olive oil

Freshly ground black pepper

12 slices chiabatta

4 ripe tomatoes

4 spring onions

Sea salt
Freshly ground black pepper
Parsley to garnish

Delicious: cod cooked with spices and mixed with mashed potato.

Soak the dried cod in cold water for 1 day, changing the water once, or buy already soaked fish. Bring the milk to the boil with all the herbs and put in the dried cod. Bring to the boil again, set aside and leave to soak for half an hour. Take out the fish, and using fingertips to detect any bones, separate the individual segments. Set the cooked fish aside.

Grind the saffron threads with a large pestle and mortar. Add the fish and mash to a smooth consistency. Blend in the boiled and peeled potato and the olive oil. Season with black pepper. Toast the bread and spread on the fish purée. Slice the tomatoes and season with salt and pepper and sprinkle with rings of spring onion. Place the dried cod crostini alongside the salad and garnish with parsley.

**60

Dried cod can normally be found in good fish-mongers
or in Spanish shops.

Cut the dried cod into manageable pieces. Soak well before preparing. Only after soaking should the fish be boiled in the seasoned milk.

Dried cod and mashed potato with garlic cream sauce

400 g / 14 oz dried cod, preferably from the back of the fish

1 litre / 32 fl oz / 4 cups whole milk

1 dried chilli
3 cloves
½ tsp white peppercorns
2 bay leaves
1 garlic clove, unpeeled, lightly crushed

20 cloves of garlic, unpeeled

4 tbsp olive oil

200 ml / 6 ½ fl oz / ¾ cup white wine fish sauce (see recipe on page 160)

For the mashed potato:
500 g / 1 lb peeled floury potatoes
80 g / 3 oz quality butter
200 ml / 6 ½ fl oz / ¾ cup whole milk
Freshly ground nutmeg
Sea salt
Freshly ground black pepper

Soak the dried cod in cold water for one day changing the water once, or buy already soaked fish. Bring the milk to the boil with all the herbs and put in the dried cod. Bring to the boil again, set aside and leave to soak for half an hour. Take out the fish, and using fingertips to detect any bones, separate the individual segments. Grind the fish in a mortar until it is very fine, at the same time, working in 3 tbsp of olive oil.

Since the dried cod is already flavoursome it harmonizes particularly well with the mashed potato. It doesn't need much more than a bit of aroma, as for example here with the garlic.

Put the garlic in an oven-proof dish, sprinkle with the rest of the olive oil and salt lightly. Bake for approximately 30 minutes in a 160° C hot oven until the garlic is very soft. Crush 4 cloves and add them to the heated white wine sauce.
In the meantime, cut the peeled potatoes in half and boil them in salt water until soft. Pour out the water and let the potatoes cool. Put them in a potato press and blend in the cold butter with a large spoon. Pour in the hot milk and season to taste with salt and nutmeg. Fold the fish into the mashed potato and add more salt and nutmeg if necessary.
Put in warmed deep dishes, garnish each with 4 cloves of roasted garlic and pour on the garlic sauce. Finish off with some freshly ground black pepper.

TIP
Make a hollow in the dried cod purée with the back of a spoon and fill with a tablespoon of good quality olive oil.

Curry of cod with papaya and roasted cauliflower florets

600 g / 21 oz cod

3 tbsp fish sauce
4 tbsp peanut oil

1 tbsp palm sugar

1 tbsp red curry paste
3 tbsp oyster sauce

100 ml / 3 ¼ fl oz / ½ cup water

1 can 400 ml / 13 fl oz / 2 cups unsweetened coconut milk

200 g / 7 oz papaya cut in pieces

120 g / 4 oz cauliflower florets

100 g / 3 ½ oz fresh peas

When buying the papaya make sure it is not too ripe or it will fall apart while cooking.

Cut the cod into bite size pieces and marinate in the fish sauce.
Heat half of the peanut oil and dissolve the palm sugar in it. Lightly roast the curry paste in the oil and add the oyster sauce and water. Let reduce and add the coconut milk. Add the marinated fish and papaya to the sauce and let simmer lightly for 3 minutes.
In the meantime, sauté the cauliflower florets on all sides in the rest of the olive oil for about 5 minutes until golden. Mix in the raw peas. Add to the fish curry and leave to marinate for a while.

TIP
Serve with basmati rice and sprinkle the curry with either Thai basil, or coriander or fine strips of lemon leaves according to preference. Cod is well suited for this dish because its texture holds the sauce well.

** 35

Spicy herb-milk hake with chilli oil and steamed rice

8 pieces hake pieces, 100 g / 3 ½ oz each
scales scraped

2 litres / 32 fl oz / 8 cups whole milk

3 dried chilli
3 bay leaves
3 sprigs of thyme

2 shallots, peeled and cut in rings

1 tsp fennel seeds

1 tsp white peppercorns

5 whole cloves

Sea salt

1 small bottle chilli oil – from an Asian
food shop

1 tsp red chilli flakes

Simple yet refined: hake cooked in
seasoned milk is mild and has a
well-rounded flavour.

Great compliments: hake and milk
seasoned with bay leaves and herbs

150 g / 5 oz long grain rice

20 g / ¾ oz butter

1 peeled white onion

2 bay leaves
6 cloves

300 ml / 9 ½ fl oz / 1 ¼ cups fish
or vegetable stock

Heat the milk in a wide pot.
Add the dried chillies, bay leaves, thyme sprigs,
cut shallots, fennel seeds, pepper and cloves.
Season heavily with salt. The milk should taste
over-salted. Bring to the boil and put in the
horizontally cut hake pieces. Turn off the heat
and leave to poach for about 10 minutes.

In the meantime, melt the butter and heat the
long grain rice until slightly transparent. Cut
the onion in half and insert in each half, a bay
leaf and three cloves. Put into the rice and
add the liquid. Cover with a lid and steam for
about 15 minutes.
Place the rice on preheated plates, take the
hake out of the milk mixture and set on the
rice. Mix the chilli oil with the chilli flakes and
drip over the fish.

×× 35

Sautéed turbot in tarragon butter and mashed potatoes

1 Turbot 1.2 kg / 2 lb 10 oz, cleaned
with head removed

30 tbsp sunflower oil

40 g butter

2 sprigs of tarragon

Juice of ½ lemon

Sea salt
Freshly ground white pepper

4 tbsp fish stock or water

For the mashed potatoes:

500 g / 1 lb peeled floury potatoes

80 g / 3 oz quality butter

200 ml / 6 ½ fl oz / ¾ cup whole milk

Freshly ground nutmeg
Sea salt

Cut the peeled potatoes in half and cook in salt water until soft. Drain and set the potatoes aside to cool. Press them in a potato press and fold in the cold butter with a spoon. Mix in the hot milk and season with the sea salt and nutmeg.

Cut off the ridge of the fin of the turbot, wash and dry with a paper towel. Cut the piece of fish with its bones into four pieces and season with salt. Place in a non-stick pan dark side down and slowly sauté for about 5 minutes. Turn the fish over and carefully remove the dark skin with a spoon and slowly sauté for another 5 minutes. Pour the oil in the pan out and add the butter. Froth the butter and baste the fish with it. Coarsely chop the tarragon leaves and sprinkle over the fish.

Pour the lemon juice onto the turbot and baste it again with its own juices.

Add the fish stock and immediately place the fish on warmed plates with the mashed potatoes and spoon over the juices from the pan.

TIP
This dish also works well with brill or black halibut. Cooking the fish on the bone keeps it especially moist and gives its juices a flavoursome and natural taste.

**✳✳40

Salmon in vegetable-citrus marinade on potato rösti with paprika yoghourt

1 side of a salmon
with skin, 1.3 kg / 2 lb 13 oz

2 celery stalks
1 fennel bulb

2 peeled white onions

2 unwaxed oranges
1 unwaxed lemon

1 bunch of dill, finely chopped
100 g / 3 ½ oz sea salt and sugar
mixture, 1:1 ratio

2 star-anise
10 cloves
1 tsp juniper berries
1 tbsp coriander seeds

300 g / 10 ½ oz large potatoes

Freshly ground nutmeg
Sea salt

4 tbsp sunflower oil

200 g / 7 oz whole milk yoghourt

1 tsp fine chilli sauce

1 tsp lemon juice

Dice the vegetables and wash the orange and lemon in hot water before cutting them complete with the peel into small cubes. Put all the ingredients in a bowl and mix with the chopped dill, sea salt-sugar mixture and the hand ground spices. Put the salmon skin side down on a platter and cover with the vegetable marinade and then cling film. Marinate for 48 hours – turn after 24 hours. Grate the potatoes, preferably with a machine. Place in a bowl and season with sea salt and freshly-ground nutmeg. Let stand for 5 minutes and firmly press with hands. Heat oil in a non-stick pan and fry the grated-potato patties 10 cm (5 in) apart until golden brown. Cut the marinated salmon in very thin slices and serve on top of the potato rösti.
Mix the yoghourt with the chilli sauce and the lemon juice and pour some onto the salmon. Garnish with a few drops of chilli sauce.

TIP
Salmon in a vegetable marinade has a very mild and fresh taste. It can be kept in the refrigerator for several days. Any remaining pieces of salmon can be used in pasta, for salmon tartare or in a salmon and pea quiche.

**180

Put the vegetable marinade, spices and fresh herbs on the inside of the fish. After 24 hours turn the fish over and let it marinate on the other side.

Salmon in vegetable-citrus marinade on potato rösti with paprika yoghourt

Bay leaf sautéed Saint Petersfish on a bed of orange and endive

600 g / 1 lb 5 oz Saint Petersfish (dory)

12 fresh bay leaves

3 endives (chicory)

Juice of 2 oranges

150 ml / 5 fl oz / ¾ cup cream

Slices of 1 orange

60 g / 2 oz butter

Sea salt
Freshly ground white pepper
½ tsp brown sugar

The endives should be fresh and crunchy and free of brown marks. Peel the orange, remove all the white pith and slice in thin slices. Remove any pips.

Cut the Saint Pertersfish lengthwise into four pieces. Froth 40 g / 1 ¼ oz butter in a non-stick pan and add the fresh bay leaves. Salt the fish pieces and lay on top of the bay leaves. Sauté for approximately 3 minutes basting with the butter. In the meantime, cut out the stem of the endives and cut them into large pieces.
Froth the rest of the butter in a non-stick pan and sprinkle in the brown sugar. Let dissolve and then add the endives. Season with pepper and salt and cook until golden. Add the orange juice and let reduce. Pour in the cream and place the orange sections into the pan. Carefully bring to the boil, stir and add a bit more salt and pepper to taste. Arrange on preheated plates and place the fish fillets in the centre.
Garnish with bay leaves.

TIP
Serve steamed rice or parsley potatoes as a side dish. Definitely use fresh bay leaves. The unusually special aroma will surprise you.

Skin the monkfish using a knife (1), then cut off the back and tail fins with scissors (2). With a sharp knife remove the skin and any sinews (3). Only the perfectly white meat without any impurities should remain (4).

**20

Fish stock

Ingredients for 2 litres / 64 fl oz of stock

1 kg / 2lb 3 oz fish carcasses*, soaked

1 white onion, peeled
3 shallots, peeled
½ bulb of fennel
2 celery stalks

3 garlic cloves, unpeeled, slighthy crushed

20 g / ¾ oz butter
2 tbsp sunflower oil

250 ml / 8 fl oz / 1 cup dry white wine
50 ml / 1 ½ fl oz / ¼ cup Noilly Prat
2 ½ litres / 80 fl oz / 10 cups cold water

1 sprig of thyme
2 bay leaves
3 basil leaves
A few parsley and basil leaf sprigs

10 ground white peppercorns
¼ tsp fennel seeds

2 lemon slices

20 g / ¾ oz coarse sea salt

*Preferably only from white fish such as sole, turbot, brill, catfish or monkfish.

To make a good fish stock it is best to use the bones
and remains of fish such as sole, brill, turbot, sea bass
or monkfish. Simmering on a low heat will release all their
flavour. Wash well to get rid of any blood or other impurities.

Fish stock

Carcasses from white meat fish are best for making fish stock: for example, sole, turbot, brill, catfish or monkfish; they give off the best aroma when cooking. Wash the carcasses well beforehand so that all blood and other impurities are removed.

Soak the carcasses for ½ an hour so that the blood is completely washed away to avoid the broth becoming murky. Dice the vegetables coarsely and sauté in butter and oil (1). Then add the spices, salt, bay and basil leaves as well as the parsley and sauté so that they can release their flavours (2). Add the soaked fish carcasses and stir (3). Splash with the white wine and Noilly Prat and add the cold water and bring slowly to a boil (4). Skim off any foam that forms, add the lemon slices and let simmer for 15 minutes (5 and 6). Pour the stock through a sieve and use it for soups or sauces.

TIP
The fish broth will keep in the refrigerator for about 5 days and can also be frozen.

Poached bows of sole with champagne sauce and caviar

8 fillets of sole

20 g / ¾ oz French butter

50 ml / 1 ½ fl oz / ¼ cup sparkling wine or champagne

Sea salt

200 ml / 6 ½ fl oz / ¾ cup white wine fish sauce (see recipe on page 160)

1 tbsp whipped cream

100 g / 3 ½ oz caviar

Important in preparation: lay the strips of sole in the generously buttered casserole dish, brush them with butter, salt lightly and put covered in the oven.

Lightly salt the fillets of sole and fold the ends together into 8 cm (4 in) long packets. Coat an ovenproof dish with butter and lay the sole packets in with the ends face down. Brush the sole with the rest of the butter and douse with the sparkling wine or champagne. Cover with wax paper and bake in a preheated 160° C oven for about 10 minutes.
In the meantime, fold the whipped cream into the white wine sauce and pour it into the baking dish around the sole packets and top each with a dab of caviar.

TIP
Serve with champagne and, if desired, white rice. The rice will absorb the sauce beautifully.

*** 45

White wine fish sauce

Ingredients for 2 l of sauce for 6-8 people

1 shallot, peeled

20 g / ¾ oz butter

200 ml / 6 ½ fl oz / ¾ cup dry white
wine or champagne

50 ml / 1 ½ fl oz / ¼ cup Noilly Prat

1 litre / 32 fl oz fish stock

250 g / 9 oz cream

200 g / 7 oz crème fraîche

A few drops of lemon juice

Pinch of cayenne pepper

30 g /1 oz cold butter cut into slices

Sea salt

Sauté the finely sliced shallots in butter (1). Add the white
wine or champagne and the Noilly Prat and allow to nearly
fully evaporate (2 and 3). Add the fish stock (4) and
reduce to a syrupy consistency, thus concentrating the
flavours. Add the cream and the crème fraîche and bring
to a slow boil (5). Remove from the heat and season to
taste with cayenne pepper, lemon juice and salt.
Add the cold butter and blend with a hand mixer (6).
Pour the sauce into a fine sieve and serve with steamed
or sautéed fish fillets.

TIP
This basic sauce can be altered in a refined manner
simply by adding other ingredients such as herbs, mustard,
tomato paste or mushrooms. Make this amount for four
people as well because there are never any left overs
of a good sauce.

*** 55

Baked whole grouper on a bed of cherry tomatoes, aubergine and green peppers

*** 90

For 6-8 people:

1 large grouper, 2 ½ kg / 5 lbs

1 sliced lemon

2 aubergines

500 g / 1 lb peeled potatoes

250 g / 8 oz small green peppers – Spanish "pimientos de padrón"

250 g / 8 oz skinned cherry tomatoes

6 tbsp extra virgin olive oil

Coarse sea salt
Freshly ground black pepper

10 basil leaves
A few light celery stalk leaves

Scrape off the scales of the grouper, clean it and cut out the gills with scissors. Cut off the back and belly fins. Dry with a paper towel. Cut into the back of the fish about 1 cm (½ in) starting from the tail fin and moving towards the head. This allows the heat to better enter the thickest part and later facilitates filleting the fish. Make a slit into the skin on the sides every 2 to 3 cm (1 to 1 ½ in). Salt the fish inside and out and stuff it with the lemon slices. Cook the fish in 2 tbsp of olive oil in a large oval pan on high heat for a few minutes and then place grilled side up on a large baking sheet.
Cut the potatoes and aubergines in half and then into smaller pieces. Sauté the potatoes in a large pan in 2 tbsp olive oil and then add salt. Take them out of the pan and sauté the aubergine and the small peppers in the rest of the oil and salt them. Put the potatoes, aubergine, green peppers and the raw tomatoes around the fish. Add black pepper and place in the preheated 200° C oven. Bake for approximately 30 minutes basting regularly with the juices from the pan. Shortly before removing from the oven sprinkle the basil and celery leaves over the fish and baste again.

TIP
Put the whole baking sheet in the middle of the table. Everyone can choose the part of the fish they want most and has fun doing so.

Sea urchin

The tongue of the sea urchin can be removed
easily with the help of a small spoon. It is wise to
wear gloves when opening the sea urchin so as
not to prick your fingers.

Sea urchin sauce

In order to open the sea urchins easily, you will need good kitchen scissors.

6 large sea urchins

20 g / ¾ oz butter

2 small shallots, peeled
1 garlic clove, peeled
¼ fennel bulb

1 ripe tomato

1 bay leaf
1 sprig of thyme

50 ml / 1 ½ fl oz / ¼ cup cognac
50 ml / 1 ½ fl oz / ¼ cup white port

250 ml / 8 fl oz / 1 cup cream
250 ml / 8 fl oz / 1 cup crème fraîche

Pinch of cayenne pepper
Sea salt

TIP
Should the sea urchins not be full of water, fish stock can be used to replace the missing liquid. Otherwise the sauce will lack taste.

Cut a circle in the bottom of the sea urchin with scissors and remove. Pour the sea urchin water through a sieve into a bowl and carefully take out the small orange tongue with a mocha spoon and keep cool.
Melt the butter and lightly sauté the sliced shallots, garlic and fennel bulb without letting them brown. Cut the tomato into large pieces and add it along with the bay leaf and thyme. Douse with cognac and white port and let reduce. Add the strained sea urchin water and reduce almost entirely. Pour in the cream and crème fraîche and season to taste with the cayenne pepper. Blend with a hand mixer and put in another casserole dish. Add half the sea urchin tongues to the sauce and if necessary season with a bit of salt. Warm the other half in the sauce and put on top of the cooked fish fillet. The sea urchin sauce tastes best with brill or halibut on a bed of spinach or with scallops.

✳✳✳45

166

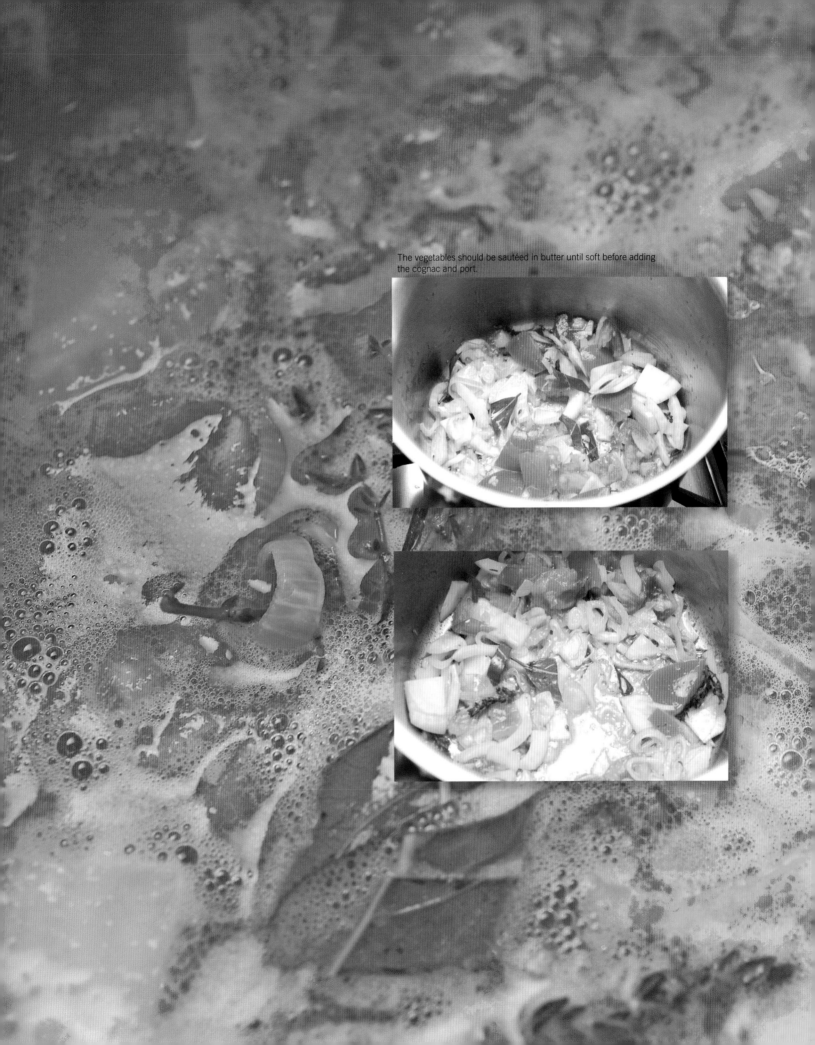

The vegetables should be sautéed in butter until soft before adding the cognac and port.

Broiled sea urchin
with brill fillets

8 fresh sea urchins

250 g / 9 oz brill fillets cut into strips

10 g / ⅓ oz butter

Pinch of cayenne pepper
Sea salt

2 egg yolks

50 ml / 1 ½ fl oz / ¼ cup dry white wine

200 ml / 6 ½ fl oz / ¾ cup sea urchin sauce
(see recipe on page 166)

1 tbsp whipped cream

Cut a circle in the bottom of the sea urchin
with scissors and remove. Pour the sea urchin
water through a sieve into a bowl and carefully
take out the small orange tongue with a mocha
spoon and keep cool. Wash out the sea urchin
shells well and place them upside-down on a
baking sheet covered with sea salt.

Melt the butter and briefly place the strips of
brill in the non-stick pan first on one side and
then the other.
Season with cayenne pepper and salt, and
place in the sea urchin shells.
In the meantime, in a double boiler beat the
egg yolk and white wine into a froth. Bring the
sea urchin sauce to the boil and add the rest of
the sea urchin tongues. Carefully fold in the egg
and the whipped cream. Fill into the sea urchin
shells and broil in a preheated oven until golden.
Take out of the oven and serve immediately on
plates coated in sea salt.

Cut the sea urchin around the opening with
scissors and preserve the juice. Lift out the
small orange coloured tongue with a spoon.

TIP
When buying the sea urchins, take an extra
one or two just in case one of the others still
has only a very small tongue.

∗∗∗35

Sea urchin soup with crème fraîche and chervil

8 fresh sea urchins

20 g / ¾ oz butter

2 small peeled shallots
1 garlic clove, peeled
¼ fennel bulb

1 ripe tomato

1 bay leaf
1 sprig of thyme

50 ml / 1 ½ fl oz / ¼ cup cognac
50 ml / 1 ½ fl oz / ¼ cup white port
½ litre / 16 fl oz / 2 cups fish stock

250 ml / 8 fl oz / 1 cup cream
250 ml / 8 fl oz / 1 cup crème fraîche

Pinch of cayenne pepper

1 tbsp whipped cream

1 tbsp chervil leaves

Sea salt

Sea urchins are not only a delight by themselves. They can be prepared in many ways, as here in a soup.

Cut a circle in the bottom of the sea urchin with scissors and remove. Pour the sea urchin water through a sieve into a bowl and carefully take out the small orange tongue with a mocha spoon and keep cool.

Melt the butter and sauté the sliced shallots, garlic and fennel bulb without letting them turn brown. Coarsely chop the tomatoes and put them into the pan together with the chopped bay leaf and thyme. Add the cognac and the white port and let reduce. Then add the strained juice from the sea urchin and the fish stock and let reduce down to half the amount. Add the cream and crème fraîche and season to taste with the cayenne pepper. Blend with a hand mixer and put into a deep casserole dish. Put half the sea urchin tongues in the soup, if desired add salt, and put the other half directly on the bottom of the preheated soup bowls. Add the whipped cream to the hot soup and pour immediately into the soup bowls and garnish with the chervil leaves.

TIP
This is a very delicate soup in which the sea urchin taste is easily recognizable. Small pieces of monkfish or steamed salmon can also be added to the bowls before pouring in the finished soup.

*** 40

Monkfish medallions on roasted artichokes with diced potatoes and red wine butter sauce

1 kg / 2 lbs 3 oz monkfish, cleaned and skinned

2 tbsp sunflower oil

10 g / ⅓ oz butter

1 tsp red hibiscus salt

12 small artichokes

3 medium floury potatoes, peeled

8 tbsp olive oil

Sea salt
Freshly ground black pepper

1 tbsp finely chopped parsley

For the red wine butter sauce:

250 ml / 8 fl oz / 1 cup heavy red wine

50 ml / 1 ½ fl oz / ¼ cup red port

1 tbsp light cream
150 g / 5 oz butter

Clean the artichokes, remove the stalks and cut into pieces. Wash in lemon water and drip dry. Heat half the olive oil and sauté the artichokes. Season with sea salt and black pepper. Heat the other half of the oil in another non-stick pan and fry the 1 cm (½ in) diced potatoes until golden and crisp and then salt them. When done, add the chopped parsley. Combine the potatoes with the artichokes, put them in a sieve and let them drain. Then put them all back in the pan to keep warm.

To make the red wine butter sauce, mix the wine and the port in a tall casserole or pot and reduce down to one fifth. Add the cream. Blend in the cold thinly sliced butter by rotating the pot. Season with sea salt and pepper. The sauce should not cook any more and cannot be kept for long.

Cut the monkfish with the bone in 2 cm (1 in) thick slices and sauté briefly on one side in sunflower oil in a hot pan and then turn. Add the butter and continue to cook, occasionally basting with the butter.

Arrange the artichoke potato mixture on preheated plates and place the monkfish medallions on top. Pour the red wine butter sauce around the medallions and at the very end season the fish with hibiscus salt.

TIP
Should you not find any hibiscus salt, use any other herbed salt. Hibiscus salt suits this dish well because it is slightly acidic and its colour matches beautifully.

***

Salmon filled cucumbers with dill sauce

4 medium cucumbers
½ bunch of dill
10 g / ¾ oz butter
100 ml / 3 ¼ fl oz / ½ cup fish stock or water
200 ml / 6 ½ fl oz / ¾ cup white wine
fish sauce (see recipe on page 160)

For the salmon filling:
250 g / 9 oz raw salmon fillet, skinned
2 cl / 6 ½ fl oz / ¾ cup Noilly Prat
2 egg yolks
200 ml / 6 ½ oz / ¾ cup cream
Sea salt
Pinch of cayenne pepper
Juice of ½ lemon
1 tbsp finely chopped dill tips

A small trick to keep the salmon filled cucumber boats from tipping over: even off the curve of the cucumber. Then put them in the casserole dish, fill with purée, add the fish stock and cook in a preheated oven.

Cut the salmon into ½ cm (¼ in) cubes, salt them and add the Noilly Prat. Put in a freezer for about half an hour. Purée the slightly frozen salmon along with the egg yolks in a blender. Mix in the cream, a small amount at a time and transfer to a cold bowl. Season to taste with cayenne pepper and lemon juice and blend in the dill.
Peel the cucumbers, cut them in half and scrape out the seeds with a small spoon.

Sprinkle the cucumbers with a bit of the dill and salt lightly. Put the salmon filling in an icing bag and fill into the cucumbers. Place in a buttered ovenproof dish and pour the stock or water over the cucumbers.
Place in a 180° C preheated oven covered with wax paper for about 20 minutes. Bring the white wine sauce to the boil and blend again with a hand mixer until frothy.
Place two halves of the cucumber on each plate and douse with the white wine sauce. Serve with steamed rice (see recipe on page 140).

*** 45

Salmon filled cucumbers
with dill sauce

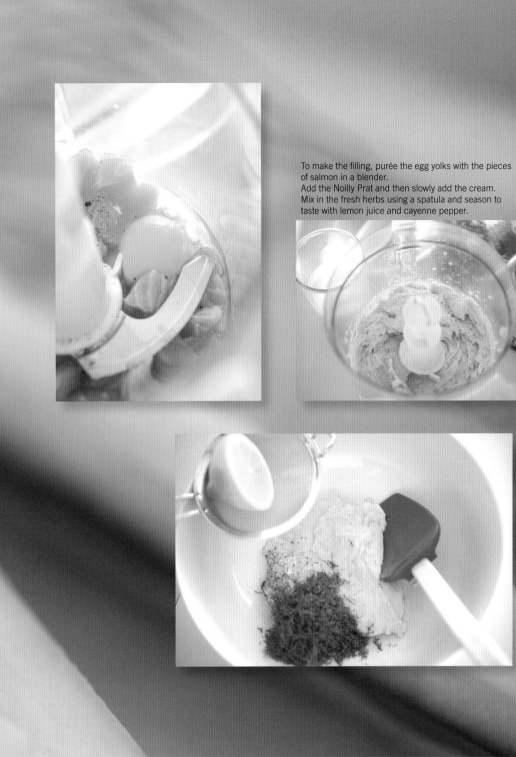

To make the filling, purée the egg yolks with the pieces of salmon in a blender.
Add the Noilly Prat and then slowly add the cream.
Mix in the fresh herbs using a spatula and season to taste with lemon juice and cayenne pepper.

Turbot fillet with tomato-mustard crust on a bed of spring leeks and white wine sauce

4 turbot fillets 200 g / 7 oz each

8 plum tomatoes, peeled, quartered and seeds removed

1 tsp coarse Meaux mustard

2 tbsp extra virgin olive oil

2 bunches of spring leeks

20 g / ¾ oz butter

Sea salt
Pinch of powdered icing sugar
Freshly ground white pepper
Freshly ground nutmeg

50 ml / 1 ½ fl oz / ¼ cup fish stock or water

½ bunch of chopped chervil leaves

200 ml / 6 ½ fl oz / ¾ cup white wine fish sauce (see recipe on page 160)

This dish is easy to prepare in advance: place the fish on the vegetables and at the last moment place the dish in the preheated oven.

Heat a tablespoon of olive oil and add the tomato quarters. Season with sea salt, icing sugar and white pepper. Place immediately on a plate to cool. Cut off the stem and upper leaves of the leeks and wash well. Cut in diagonal slices and sauté in frothed butter. Season to taste with sea salt and nutmeg and put in an ovenproof dish. Salt the turbot fillets and spread with the mustard mixed with 1 tbsp of olive oil. Place them on top of the bed of leeks and the sautéed tomatoes on top of the fillets. Spread with the rest of the mustard-oil mixture and add the fish stock or water.
Cover with waxed paper and place in the 180° C preheated oven. Bake for about 10 minutes. The fish is done as soon as the liquid has evaporated.

Take out of the oven.
Bring the white wine sauce to the boil, combine with the chervil leaves and pour onto the spring leeks. This way the sauce takes on the taste of the leeks and you can serve the food in the casserole dish.

✳✳✳ 60

Lobster pot au feu in cognac tomato sauce

1 large live lobster, preferably European,
about 1 kg / approx. 2 lb
(or 2 of 500 g / approx. 1 lb each)

4 tbsp olive oil
60 g / 2 oz butter

½ garlic clove, diced
2 small shallots, diced and peeled
100 g / 3 ½ oz diced carrot
100 g / 3 ½ oz diced celery
100 g / 3 ½ oz diced fennel bulb
2 bay leaves
2 sprigs of thyme

1 tbsp tomato paste
300 ml / 9 ¾ fl oz / 1 ¼ cups tomato juice

100 ml / 3 ¼ fl oz / ½ cup cognac
100 ml / 3 ¼ fl oz / ½ cup dry white wine
500 ml / 16 fl oz / 2 cups crayfish or fish stock

The European lobster, also known as blue lobster, has the best meat. This is how it tastes best: boil quickly in hot water and then cut it into pieces and sauté in oil.

Cut the lobster in half with a large knife. Cut off the tail and slice between the joints of the tail to make medallions. Cut the end part of the tail in half. Break open the lobster claws with the back of the knife and cut open the claw joints.
Heat the oil in a pan, season the lobster pieces with salt and pepper, and sauté them on both sides. Add and froth the butter.
Put in the diced garlic and shallots and sauté until transparent. Add the diced vegetables, chopped bay leaves and thyme sprig and season again with sea salt and pepper. When the vegetables are nearly done, add the tomato purée and roast lightly. Pour in the tomato juice and allow to evaporate.

Add, and then reduce, the cognac and white wine. Add the crayfish stock and leave to simmer for another 5 minutes until the sauce has a thick consistency.
Arrange on plates and serve with steamed rice (see recipe on page 140).

*** 45

The pot should be large enough so that the lobster and the vegetables cook evenly in the pot au feu.

Creole style skate wing with couscous

2 skate wings on the bone 500 g / approx. 1 lb each

6 tbsp peanut oil

1 aubergine
1 yellow pepper
2 red peppers
2 white onions, peeled

1 cinnamon stick

½ tsp ground turmeric

1 tbsp garam masala

3 garlic cloves, chopped

400 g / 14 oz peeled tomatoes with juice

500 ml / 16 fl oz / 2 cups fish stock or water

2 limes

Coriander to garnish

For the couscous:

300 g / 10 ½ oz couscous

700 g / 25 oz clear chicken or vegetable stock

½ tsp saffron threads

4 tbsp extra virgin olive oil

5 large mint leaves, cut into strips

200 g / 7 oz whole milk yoghourt

Juice of ½ lemon

Freshly ground black pepper
Sea salt

Clean the skate wings and dry with paper towels.
Remove any remaining pieces of skin and cut the fish
into approximately 8 x 8 cm (3 x 3 in) pieces. Season
with salt and pepper and sauté in a large pot in half
of the peanut oil.
Take out and set aside.
Cut off the stems of the aubergines.
Cut the peppers in half, cut off the stems and remove
the white parts from inside and then wash them. Cut
the onions, aubergines and peppers into 4 cm (2 in)
pieces and cut the lime into eighths.
Heat the rest of the peanut oil in the large pot and
first roast the cinnamon, turmeric and garam masala
to intensify the taste. Add the chopped garlic and
vegetables, season with salt and roast.
Add the grilled skate, whole tomatoes with juice and
the fish stock. Put the lime sections on top and cover
with a lid.
Leave to simmer for about 20 minutes. Stir carefully so
as not to damage the fish.
In the meantime, bring the chicken stock with the
saffron threads to the boil and pour over the couscous.
Stir with a long-pronged fork and leave to cook for
20 minutes, stirring occasionally to fluff up the
couscous.
Fold in the olive oil and mint leaves.
Place the couscous like a wreath on a large platter
or in a bowl and put the skate ragout in the centre.
Garnish with coriander leaves. Mix the yoghourt with
the lemon juice, black pepper and some sea salt and
serve with the ragout.

*** 75

Cream of shellfish soup